Mastermind

Exercises in Critical Thinking, Grades 4–6

**If you enjoyed this book, you might find
these other Good Year Books® useful:**

FANTASTIC READING: Stories and Activities for Grades 5–8
Isaac Asimov, Martin H. Greenberg, and David Clark Yeager

I'M AN EXPERT: Motivating Independent Study Projects
Mel Cebulash

THE POETRY CORNER
Arnold Cheyney

SOLVING PROBLEMS KIDS CARE ABOUT: Math Skills and Word Problems
Randall J. Souviney

THINK & WRITE
Hilarie N. Staton

WHO SAYS YOU CAN'T TEACH SCIENCE?
Alan Ticotsky

THE WHOLE COSMOS CATALOG OF SCIENCE ACTIVITIES
Joe Abruscato and Jack Hassard

WORD WIZARDRY: An Enchantment of Word Games, Puzzles, and Activities
Linda Shevitz

WRITE UP A STORM:
Creative Writing Ideas and Activities for the Middle Grades
Linda Polon and Aileen Cantwell

THE WRITING DISCOVERY BOOK: New Ways to Improve Writing Skills
David Clark Yeager

For information about these or any Good Year Books®,
please write to

Good Year Books
Scott, Foresman and Company
1900 East Lake Avenue
Glenview, Illinois 60025

Mastermind

Exercises in Critical Thinking, Grades 4–6

Zacharie J. Clements
University of Vermont

Richard R. Hawkes
University of Northern Iowa

Scott, Foresman and Company
Glenview, Illinois   London

ISBN 0-673-16653-8

1 2 3 4 5 6-MAL-89 88 87 86 85

ACKNOWLEDGMENTS

We extend sincere thanks to the following contributors. Without their help this project could not have succeeded: Nancy Gilbert, typist, editor, duplicator, and more; Susan Eddy, graduate assistant and super material creator; Terri Bailey, typist, editor, and more; Jan Hawkes, editor, supporter, friend, and confidante; Bonnie Mansfield, activities creator and friend.

We are also grateful for the careful reviewing done by Deborah Soglin, David Yeager, Peggy Christensen, and Janet Lovelady.

Zacharie J. Clements
Richard R. Hawkes

CONTENTS

INTRODUCTION

The classroom activities in this book are designed to stimulate students who periodically need a challenge— to foster the development of critical-thinking skills for the Talented and Gifted learner in elementary school.*

Mastermind activities strive to accomplish three primary objectives:
1. Provide students with supplemental work aimed at developing thinking skills.
2. Identify areas of need through examining student performance in the areas of thinking-skills development.
3. Provide readily available activities that assist the teacher in expanding thinking-skills development or that assist in reinforcing identified needs or skills.

For structure, as well as a hierarchy of skills development, the activities have been grouped according to Bloom's Taxonomy of Educational Objectives. Bloom's Taxonomy divides the way people learn into three domains: the *affective domain* emphasizes feelings and emotions; the *psychomotor domain* stresses physical motor skills; and the *cognitive domain* emphasizes intellectual outcomes. Each is further subdivided into categories.

Students using this book will perform tasks in the six subcategories of the cognitive domain. The following brief explanations of each subcategory include descriptions of the types of cognitive activities performed. The categories are hierarchical, proceeding from the lowest level of cognition, knowledge, to the highest, evaluation.

Major Subcategories of the Cognitive Domain

1. *Knowledge.* Knowledge is the remembering of previously learned material. This may involve recall of a wide range of material, from specific facts to complete theories, but all that is required is the bringing to mind of appropriate information.
- *Expected student behavior:* stating, labeling, identifying, defining, matching, listing, and duplicating.
- *The student knows:* terms, facts, basic concepts, and principles

2. *Comprehension.* Comprehension is the ability to grasp the meaning of material. This may be shown by translating material from one form to another, by interpreting material, and by estimating future trends.
- *Expected student behavior:* explaining, inferring, predicting, rewriting, extending, estimating, converting, and giving summaries
- *The student can:* understand facts and principles, interpret material such as charts and graphs, and estimate future happenings based on the data

3. *Application.* Application is the ability to use learned material in new and concrete situations. This may include the application of rules, methods, concepts, principles, laws, and theories.
- *Expected student behavior:* relating, changing, computing, solving, using, manipulating, and demonstrating
- *The student can:* apply learned laws and theories, solve mathematical problems, construct graphs and charts, and use procedures correctly

4. *Analysis.* Analysis is the ability to break down material into its component parts so that its organizational structure can be understood. This may include the identification of the parts, analysis of the relationship between parts, and recognition of the organizational principles involved.
- *Expected student behavior:* diagraming, distinguishing, inferring, selecting, separating, and outlining
- *The student can:* distinguish fact from fiction, recognize assumptions, and evaluate data

---

*Although designed with Talented and Gifted (TAG) students as a primary audience, the activities in *Mastermind* can be used by any reasonably self-motivated student.

5. *Synthesis.* Synthesis is the ability to put parts together to form a new whole. This may involve the production of a unique communication, a plan of operations, or a set of abstract relations.

- *Expected student behavior:* complying, creating, composing, modifying, organizing, rearranging, designing, categorizing, summarizing, and planning
- *The student can:* create a story, integrate learning for problem solving, and develop schemes for categorizing objects

6. *Evaluation.* Evaluation is the ability to judge the value of material for a given purpose. Judgments must be based on definite criteria. Criteria may be internal (organizational) or external (relevant to a purpose), and the student may determine the criteria or be given them.

- *Expected student behavior:* criticizing, describing, contrasting, supporting, comparing, interpreting, appraising, and explaining
- *The student can:* judge whether conclusions are supported by data, judge the value of work by using standards, and check for consistency in written material

Some activities may seem too easy or may overemphasize organizational skills. These activities are so designed to (1) develop and reinforce subskills necessary to perform more difficult tasks and (2) to serve as confidence-builders for more difficult tasks. The primary objective of each category is to provide students with opportunities to develop new critical-thinking skills and reinforce those they already use.

HOW TO USE THIS BOOK

Because the activities in this book are designed around the six cognitive domain categories, they can best challenge students by being keyed, when possible, to the regular classroom curriculum. Keying can be accomplished by reviewing up-coming units in the regular curriculum and noting those areas that can best be supplemented by *Mastermind* activities.

The curriculum cross-reference form can be used to determine when certain activities are appropriate. (The Contents includes notations about basic subject matter: math activity, social studies, science, language arts, and so on.)

The activities are designed to be corrected by the teacher. An answer key appears at the end of the book. (Responsible students can also use the key to correct their own activities, but note that *all* activity answers are shown.) Each activity should be corrected and scored before another one is attempted. This system of immediate feedback helps determine whether a student should go on to the next activity or repeat the last one to raise the score. Use the student score sheet to see, at a glance, whether a student is having difficulty in a particular area. If additional tries at an activity are made, note the scores in different colors (blue = first try, red = second try, green = third try, for example). It is also a good idea to preview each section before assigning the individual activities.

At the beginning of each unit, a "Helpful Hints" section is included to provide strategies for completing the activities. Students should read through these hints before starting any activity in the unit and be encouraged to review them if they have difficulty finishing an activity.

Additional Suggestions for Using this Book

1. As a general rule, students should do no more than one activity at any level before the teacher sees the results.

2. The teacher should keep students at one activity level until they have achieved a rating of 80 percent or more.

3. The teacher should have a student do at least three activities successfully at any level before moving on to the next unit.

4. Some activities require more time than others, so beware of setting rigid time limits.

5. The activities are designed so that the student can begin and end according to the dictates of the classroom. The student need not finish a problem at one sitting.

6. Most activities can be done by more than one student. If students work together, try to pair them according to their skill levels; they need to contribute as equally as possible.

7. The teacher should give the student a raw score, for example, 10 out of 18 points, as well as a rating label, such as 100%, "Awesome"; missed 2, "Super Star"; missed 4, "Honorable Mention"; and so on. Teachers are encouraged to create a descriptive scale that fits their students.

Curriculum Cross-Reference Form

Student's name	Curriculum unit and page	*Mastermind* activity

Place the curricular area and the page number in the space provided next to each student's name. Then, in the third column, list the number of the *Mastermind* activity that will be used as a supplement for that student. Check the Contents for subject areas.

Student Score Sheet

Name _____

KNOWLEDGE	Points received	Points possible
1	_____	_____
2	_____	_____
3	_____	_____
4	_____	_____
5	_____	_____
6	_____	_____
7	_____	_____
8	_____	_____
9	_____	_____
Total points _____		

APPLICATION	Points received	Points possible
1	_____	_____
2	_____	_____
3	_____	_____
4	_____	_____
5	_____	_____
6	_____	_____
7	_____	_____
8	_____	_____
9	_____	_____
Total points _____		

COMPREHENSION	Points received	Points possible
1	_____	_____
2	_____	_____
3	_____	_____
4	_____	_____
5	_____	_____
6	_____	_____
7	_____	_____
8	_____	_____
9	_____	_____
Total points _____		

ANALYSIS	Points received	Points possible
1	_____	_____
2	_____	_____
3	_____	_____
4	_____	_____
5	_____	_____
6	_____	_____
7	_____	_____
8	_____	_____
9	_____	_____
Total points _____		

SYNTHESIS	Points received	Points possible
1	_____	_____
2	_____	_____
3	_____	_____
4	_____	_____
5	_____	_____
6	_____	_____
7	_____	_____
8	_____	_____
9	_____	_____

Total points _____

EVALUATION Teacher Comments

1 _____

2 _____

3 _____

4 _____

5 _____

6 _____

7 _____

8 _____

9 _____

OVERVIEW OF THE UNITS

Knowledge

This unit is the first of six units. It focuses on the lowest level of the thinking processes. *Knowledge* is "the ability to remember previously learned material or skills." It requires that students remember facts or even rules. The activities ask students to use information they already know, to label, define, list, or duplicate, for example.

Comprehension

The Comprehension unit focuses on the student's ability to grasp the meaning of material. Sometimes it means that the student must translate material from one form to another (from words to numbers, for example). But *comprehension* also means "the ability to predict what will happen." In this section, students are asked to explain, estimate, interpret, and summarize, for example.

Applications

This unit focuses on the student's ability to use learned material in new situations—rules, laws, and information he or she already knows. The activities ask that students add and subtract, multiply and divide, change information, and use information, for example.

Analysis

Unit IV, Analysis, requires that students break down material into its various parts so the whole structure may be better understood. Students are asked to identify parts, see how parts go together (relationships), and recognize the rules involved. They will also use laws and rules they know, solve mathematical problems, and construct graphs and charts.

Synthesis

This unit focuses on the ability to put different parts together to form a new whole. These activities involve creating a unique form of communication or developing a plan or procedures. In these activites, students are asked to rearrange, design, organize, or bring all the information together.

Evaluation

Evaluation is the highest category of thinking, the ability to judge the value of materials being used. Judgments are usually made by knowing and following specific rules.

In this final unit, students are asked to criticize, describe, support, compare, and explain. They are also asked to judge whether answers or conclusions presented can be supported by data, and to justify their judgments.

It is extremely important to let the students know that there are *no* right or wrong answers. The emphasis in evaluation is on the use of high-level thinking skills to support or document answers or solutions. The evaluation problems require that the teacher correct the students' work. The teacher should avoid giving the student right or wrong feedback; the emphasis is on the *process* used. All directions require the students to support their answers, judgments, or conclusions. The teacher should remind students that all answers are judgments and are acceptable when accompanied by a justification.

When appropriate, the answer key has suggested conclusions or solutions that can be used as guides in reviewing the students' work. The teacher is encouraged to accept the students' answers if they provide justification. The emphasis should be on the process of supporting feelings and being able to see a relationship between conclusions and the data presented.

Mastermind

Exercises in Critical Thinking, Grades 4–6

KNOWLEDGE

Helpful Hints

These activities are under the "Knowledge" category. Knowledge is "the ability to remember previously learned material or skills." These activities require you to match, label, or identify.

These activities are meant to be fun, but some are also meant to be hard, and that's why we've placed this "Helpful Hints" section first.

Here is a series of guidelines and suggestions to give you some help before you begin. These suggestions are really tools to help you understand the exercises. Read each suggestion and place a checkmark in the box, indicating you understand what we've suggested.

☐ **1.** Always start with the first activity. It's an introductory activity and should help you understand what follows. Don't skip the first activity.

☐ **2.** Read each activity carefully. Make sure you know what you're being asked to do.

☐ **3.** Some activities have examples. Study them carefully.

☐ **4.** Keep your dictionary handy and use it to look up words you don't know.

☐ **5.** Have scratch paper handy and use it to help work out solutions.

☐ **6.** If you're working on a math problem, review your work carefully. Did you add, subtract, multiply, and divide correctly?

☐ **7.** Look for any hints in the directions, such as "Use your dictionary as needed."

☐ **8.** Don't be afraid to ask a classroom friend for his or her ideas. Sometimes another student can see something you've missed.

☐ **9.** Your teacher can help. But be sure you ask your teacher a specific question. Don't just say, "I need help" or "I don't understand." Ask your teacher something about the task. Be specific and ask only *one question at a time*.

☐ **10.** If you really get stuck, stop! Put your book away and come back to the problem later.

Name _____

The Vegetable Garden

DIRECTIONS: Do you like vegetables? How much do you know about them? This activity will check your ability to *identify* vegetables from a description given. The following names of vegetables are all fairly common. See if you can match the names in column A with their description in column B.

A. Vegetables

a. tomato
b. lettuce
c. cucumber
d. potato
e. carrot
f. string bean
g. beet
h. radish
i. corn
j. cabbage
k. celery
l. onion
m. peas
n. spinach

B. Description

1. _____ deep red; its above-ground greens can be eaten when the vegetable is still young.

2. _____ crunchy to eat; light green; it grows in a stalk.

3. _____ dark green; they grow in a pod.

4. _____ dark green; what Popeye likes to eat.

5. _____ dark green skin but white on the inside, with small seeds. It is often used in making pickles.

6. _____ grows under ground and is orange. It has a green top that grows above ground.

7. _____ red on the outside, white on the inside, and it has a hot taste.

8. _____ usually it is the main part of a salad and sometimes is eaten in a sandwich. It is green.

9. _____ deep yellow; it is grown on an ear and has a green covering while growing.

10. _____ deep red; almost round in shape; is eaten plain or in salads and sometimes in sandwiches.

11. _____ grows in a head; light green; is used to make cole slaw.

12. _____ has a brown covering but is white on the inside. When you cut one up it makes you cry.

13. _____ there are two different types; one is yellow, the other green, and both are long and skinny.

14. _____ can be eaten in many ways—fried, boiled, or baked. They have a brown skin that can be peeled off but is sometimes left on. It is white on the inside.

I.1

The Proof Is in the Reading

DIRECTIONS: Some people think that proofreading is a dull activity and isn't important. Boy, are they wrong. Proofreading is a very important job. Everything that's published, like newspapers, magazines, and even this book, are read very carefully by professional proofreaders whose job it is to find errors. They read every word before it goes to press. Sometimes proofreading can even be fun because they discover funny mistakes. We've listed some sentences below that need your proofreading skills. Specifically, these sentences need to be properly capitalized. It will require you to use the rules of capitalization you've learned.

Proofreading Exercise

Draw a line under all letters that need to be capitalized.

1. did you receive a copy of the book standard proofreading practices?
2. The senator from iowa proposed the new bill.
3. the east coast will be the geographic area selected for release of our new super suds dishwasher soap.
4. when you arrive in san Francisco, call the bowens company and ask for jim johnson.
5. Many teachers belong to professional organizations like the national education association, also known as the n.e.a., or the american federation of teachers, a.f.t.

6. A luggage exhibition will be held this spring at midlands mall shopping center.
7. Only colonel Beans can solve this problem.
8. All students at our school are required to take latin and history in order to graduate.
9. three mernard television sets arrived without picture tubes.
10. the state of vermont has many beautiful places to visit.

Extra Credit

As we said before, proofreading can also be funny. Read the following sentences and change them so that they make sense.

11. Boy raced the bat to pick up the dropped hat.
12. The new students asked for the teacher to raise their questions if they had any hands.

I.2

Sports Aplenty

DIRECTIONS: The following puzzle contains names of many sports that are common to you. There are 12 in all. *Identify* as many as you can and circle them. They can be either across or up and down. When you have found as many as you can, check the answer sheet and see how you did.

A	C	Z	K	L	B	A	S	K	E	T	B	A	L	L
L	T	H	F	G	R	H	I	I	E	T	G	S	U	D
S	B	B	Z	D	U	S	O	C	C	E	R	A	R	F
M	J	A	C	T	H	X	Y	K	Z	B	Y	C	N	Z
T	A	S	Y	S	O	F	T	B	A	L	L	G	E	O
R	V	E	U	X	C	K	F	A	G	D	M	Y	P	X
V	K	B	J	E	K	X	S	L	L	Z	D	M	Q	O
O	K	A	L	W	E	Y	K	L	T	E	N	N	I	S
V	O	L	L	E	Y	B	A	L	L	H	M	A	N	W
F	S	L	J	Q	P	G	T	T	I	C	R	S	W	I
X	M	B	B	R	C	I	I	Q	C	A	D	T	E	M
Y	C	A	W	H	P	M	N	B	J	T	V	I	B	M
L	R	V	O	F	G	S	G	F	B	U	K	C	L	I
Z	N	E	P	Q	A	W	J	V	C	P	Q	S	H	N
N	O	B	A	D	M	I	T	T	O	N	A	G	D	G

I.3

The Scrambled Home

DIRECTIONS: The following scrambled words name objects and people found in and around the home. See if you can unscramble all the words and place the correct word in the space provided. We divided the words into groups to help you out. Think about the group before you try to unscramble the words. This activity uses your ability to *identify* a word by thinking about objects at home. If you know a word but aren't sure about its spelling, it's OK to look it up in a dictionary.

A. Indoor objects   **Answers**   **B. Outdoor objects**

   1. rtufurnei _____   **8.** nredag _____

   2. beatl _____   **9.** wnla _____

   3. knis _____   **10.** npicci beatl _____

   4. hcocu _____   **C. People**

   5. shacir _____   **11.** rhetom _____

   6. plam _____   **12.** tsrise _____

   7. nelvsioite _____   **13.** trobher _____

   14. etrfah _____

   15. peersheekou _____

A Word a Day

DIRECTIONS: Some people try to learn a new word every day. This helps them increase their vocabulary. Try the following words and see how many you know. Try to do it without a dictionary. See how many words you can *define*.

A Vocabulary Challenge

Look at the words on the left and match them to the best definition that follows. Place the letter of the *best* answer in the answer space.

1. cynical   (a) guaranteed   (b) without   (c) sarcastic   (d) big   _____

2. velocity   (a) help   (b) quickness of motion   (c) size   (d) shape   _____

3. acclaim   (a) part of   (b) limited   (c) applaud   (d) organized   _____

4. domestic   (a) animal   (b) worthy cause   (c) dirty   (d) tame   _____

5. patron   (a) behind   (b) criminal   (c) wood   (d) benefactor   _____

6. felon   (a) assistant   (b) childlike   (c) adult
                 (d) one who commits a crime   _____

7. tenured   (a) having a permanent position   (b) to increase
                 (c) to decrease   (d) without light   _____

8. mercenary   (a) without mercy   (b) real concern
                 (c) working only for a reward   (d) limited   _____

9. significant   (a) without praise   (b) momentous; very important
                 (c) clean   (d) underhanded   _____

10. repudiated   (a) given help   (b) disowned   (c) terminate   (d) energy   _____

11. intervene   (a) to come between   (b) to go without
                 (c) conforming   (d) private   _____

12. vigil   (a) backward   (b) an act or period of keeping watch
                 (c) conspiracy   (d) to respond   _____

I.5

The Great Outdoors

DIRECTIONS: The following puzzle contains names of many things commonly found outdoors. There are 17 in all. *Identify* the words by circling them. They can be either across or up and down. When you have found all you can, check the answer sheet and see how you did.

R	K	M	C	S	X	Y	K	V	T	U	C	Q	T	P
P	D	L	M	W	A	L	E	X	R	D	I	R	T	F
I	N	A	Y	Z	J	B	W	J	E	G	D	O	H	S
C	L	W	T	Z	U	I	V	I	E	A	H	C	R	I
N	B	N	A	V	G	R	A	S	S	H	I	K	J	N
I	A	M	U	N	A	T	B	K	L	E	E	S	Q	S
C	H	O	S	E	R	C	S	Y	V	M	G	N	O	E
T	O	W	B	O	D	Z	L	W	F	M	P	R	K	C
A	L	E	A	V	E	S	F	D	Y	F	Z	A	O	T
B	W	R	P	K	N	G	X	G	Q	H	Y	K	I	S
L	J	C	V	R	X	W	E	A	Z	W	E	E	D	S
E	M	O	U	N	T	A	I	N	S	O	I	N	N	J
D	U	Q	E	R	Y	F	X	F	L	O	W	E	R	S
I	P	T	S	G	D	R	S	H	Q	D	B	K	C	O
V	E	G	E	T	A	B	L	E	S	S	M	P	U	L

I.6

Scrambled School

DIRECTIONS: How much do you know about school? The following scrambled words are all common terms we use in school. See if you can unscramble all the words and place the correct word in the answer space. We divided the words into groups to help you out. Think about the groups before trying to unscramble and *identify* the school-related words.

A. People — Answer

1. tosuidanc _____

2. larinpcip _____

3. heatcres _____

4. ustetnds _____

B. Subjects

5. hmta _____

6. nrwitig _____

7. ymg _____

8. igpllesn _____

9. ideragn _____

C. Objects — Answer

10. lelb _____

11. skde _____

12. npelci _____

13. npe _____

14. pprae _____

15. sokbo _____

16. loosch _____

17. hirca _____

18. lcoksc _____

D. Times of the day

19. nuhcl _____

20. sescre _____

I.7

The Marvelous Machine

DIRECTIONS: A physiologist is a scientist who studies the human body and the way its parts function. He or she seeks scientific explanations for the ways our bodies work. The human body is the most complicated organism known. Let's see how much you know about your body. You will be asked to *define* some important words and terms used by the physiologist.

Match the medical or scientific term on the left with the explanation or definition on the right. Try it first without your dictionary. Use your dictionary only when you are really stumped.

Terms

a. skeletal system
b. ligaments
c. circulatory system
d. respiratory system
e. gastrointestinal system
f. enzymes
g. diaphragm
h. chromosomes
i. endocrine system
j. saliva
k. hemoglobin
l. hormones
m. central nervous system
n. autonomic nervous system
o. esophagus

Explanations/Descriptions

1. _____ nourishes cells and cell respiration

2. _____ the chemical control system of the body

3. _____ tissue that holds bones together

4. _____ the system that controls your thinking and voluntary actions

5. _____ the food passage between the throat and the stomach

6. _____ the body system responsible for the digestion of food

7. _____ the muscle that causes the lungs to expand

8. _____ chemicals secreted by the body that cause other chemical reactions to occur

9. _____ the first digestive juice

10. _____ gives blood its red color

11. _____ contains the heredity factors

12. _____ the organs that perform the function of breathing

13. _____ chemicals that help growth and body development

14. _____ the system of bones in the body

15. _____ controls the internal organs that act involuntarily, like the lungs

I.8

Name _____

What's in a Word?

DIRECTIONS: Can you figure out words from scrambled letters? Homophones, or homonyms, are words that sound alike but have different meanings. Change a pair of words that are *not* related into a pair of homonyms by changing the order of the letters.

EXAMPLE: sleep   _____peels_____

leaps   _____peals_____

1. seal   _____

ails   _____

2. sweat   _____

waits   _____

3. teem   _____

mate   _____

4. rose   _____

oars   _____

5. feel   _____

leaf   _____

6. sleet   _____

least   _____

An antonym, on the other hand, is a word that means the *opposite of* a given word. Here are some more scrambled words. Can you figure out the words and their antonyms?

EXAMPLE: vase   _____save_____

sue   _____use_____

7. teem   _____

rapt   _____

8. won   _____

tern   _____

9. den   _____

tarts   _____

10. owls   _____

fats   _____

11. buys   _____

lied   _____

12. woe   _____

yap   _____

I.9

COMPREHENSION

Helpful Hints

These activities are under the "Comprehension" category. Comprehension means "the ability to grasp the meaning of the material." You will be asked to do things like predict, estimate, or rewrite.

Please look over the *hints* that follow before you tackle the activities. The suggestions below will give you some things to think about before you begin. The activities are fun but can also be difficult if you aren't careful.

Read each of the following suggestions. Then place a checkmark in the boxes provided to show you understand what you're being asked to do.

☐ **1.** Start with the first activity. Don't skip ahead.

☐ **2.** Have scratch paper handy and give yourself plenty of room so you can see your own work.

☐ **3.** Read the directions carefully. Make sure you understand what you're being asked to do.

☐ **4.** Underline the name of the skill you're asked to use.
Example: <u>estimate</u> the score.

☐ **5.** If the activity is a math problem, look carefully at the skills you need to use. Do you need to add, subtract, multiply, or divide? Write what you need to do on your scratch paper.

☐ **6.** Look for the hints in the directions, such as *add,* then *subtract,* to get the correct answer.

☐ **7.** Some of the activities have examples; study them carefully.

☐ **8.** If it's OK with your teacher, ask a friend for his or her ideas. Sometimes another student can see something you've missed.

☐ **9.** Ask your teacher for help. But be sure to ask a specific question. Don't just say, "I'm stuck." Think about your question before you go to your teacher.

☐ **10.** If you're really stuck, stop. Put your book away and come back to it later.

The Name's the Same

DIRECTIONS: In the following math problems, first find the correct answer to the listed problem and put the answer in the box provided. Then, using the answer, come up with a problem that has the same answer. Your new problem must use a two-digit multiplication equation.

EXAMPLE: $8 + 8 =$ ⬜ 16 $= 4 \times 4$ or 16×1 or 2×8. Try to get all the possible answers.

1. $10 + 10 =$ ⬜ = _____

2. $12 - 6 =$ ⬜ = _____

3. $48 \div 4 =$ ⬜ = _____

4. $99 \div 3 =$ ⬜ = _____

5. $24 - 3 =$ ⬜ = _____

6. $64 - 40 =$ ⬜ = _____

7. $125 - 100 =$ ⬜ = _____

8. $6 + 6 + 24 =$ ⬜ = _____

9. $50 - 10 \times 1 =$ ⬜ = _____

10. $20 \times 4 - 20 =$ ⬜ = _____

11. $20 \times 2 + 5 =$ ⬜ = _____

12. $100 - 50 \times 1 =$ ⬜ = _____

13. $30 \times 3 \times 1 =$ ⬜ = _____

14. $50 \times 3 - 75 \times 1 =$ ⬜ = _____

15. $33 \times 3 - 69 + 2 =$ ⬜ = _____

II.1

Another Way

DIRECTIONS: In today's world it is sometimes important to be able to change measurements from the U.S. system, or English system, to the metric system. The problems below are typical situations in which conversion from metric to English is needed. Let's see how you are at converting one system to the other. (If you need some help, most large dictionaries have metric tables in the back of the book. Proper use of a table is also important. Be careful.) These problems require you to use many skills. Good luck.

EXAMPLE: John bought a 3.785-*liter* bottle of milk, which equals <u>1</u> gallon.

1. The carpenter measured a board exactly 1 *meter* long and converted the measurement

to _____ feet.

2. Mom's recipe called for 1 *liter* of milk,

or _____ quarts of milk.

3. The truck driver traveled 45 *kilometers,*

or _____ miles in one day.

4. The farmer ordered 75 *pounds* of seeds. The bags came in *kilograms*, not pounds. How many bags did he need to buy to get at least 75

pounds? _____ How many pounds did he end up buying?

_____

5. The jeweler ordered 3 *decagrams* of gold. How much did this order weigh in ounces?

_____ How many *grams* did he

order? _____

6. The chemicals arrived in *hectoliter* containers, which equal how many gallons? (to the closest

gallon) _____

7. How fast can you travel in *kilometers* per hour without exceeding the speed limit of 55

miles per hour? _____ (Round off to the closest kilometer without going over 55 m.p.h.)

8. The cloth came in a roll 39.37 *inches* long. How many *decimeters* is that?

_____ How many

centimeters? _____

9. Mr. Johnson purchased a European car that weighed 2 *metric tons*. His license application asked for the car's weight in pounds. What did

he write down? _____

10. If you are on the track team, how far in yards would you run the following races?

100-meter sprint = _____ yards

110-meter hurdle = _____ yards

1500-meter run = _____ yards

II.2

The Vitamin Alphabet

DIRECTIONS: Vitamins play an important part in the proper functioning of our bodies. Too much of a single vitamin can be harmful, and the lack of a vitamin has some harmful effects on our bodies. Some of the more common vitamins and their importance to our bodies are listed in the chart below. Read them carefully. Then decide which vitamin you might prescribe, if you were a doctor, to help with the difficulty described. (We want you to know that many problems cannot be helped by simply prescribing vitamins and that no pills, including vitamins, should ever be taken without a doctor's approval.) If you need to, use your dictionary.

Vitamins

A	B_1	C	D	K	B_{12}	B_2
fights infection; prevents blindness	stimulates appetite; helps promote growth	promotes healing; maintains healthy body tissue	helps build strong bones and teeth	helps our blood coagulate	prevents anemia; helps normal growth	promotes clear vision; helps cells use oxygen

Based on the chart, what vitamin would you prescribe for the following cases. Write your choice of the vitamin or vitamins in the spaces provided.

1. what a 13-year-old boy who isn't growing as fast as the other kids might need

_____

2. what the 13-year-old boy mentioned above might need to increase his appetite

_____

3. what the dentist might want young children

to get lots of _____

4. will help the healing process

_____

5. prescribed to help a patient with

blood-clotting problems _____

6. what the eye doctor likes growing children to have the proper amounts of

_____

7. helps your body ward off infection

_____

8. helps keep a 12-year-old girl's bones strong

and healthy _____

9. helps our body use oxygen

_____

10. prescribed by the doctor, along with medication, to help a person who has cuts and sores that aren't healing properly

_____

II.3

The Big Eaters

DIRECTIONS: Study the chart shown below carefully. This chart is called a *line graph*. This line graph shows the number of pizzas purchased by the coaches for the football team at North Jr. High School. Do you see a pattern?

Pizzas Eaten by the Football Team

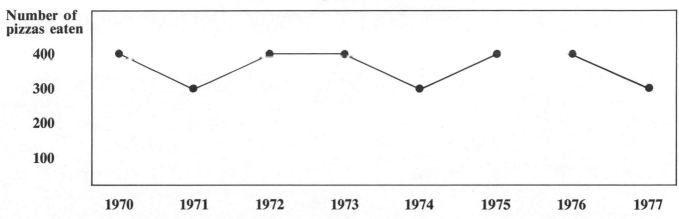

If you've identified the pattern, complete the chart below. You must predict the number of pizzas the coaches will be buying for the next eight years.

II.4

Measuring Up

DIRECTIONS: Let's work some more with the metric system. Estimating is an important skill in any system of measurement. The following matching game is designed to see how well you comprehend the metric system. Use your knowledge of the weights of each object listed to match it to the metric descriptions given. You might have to use your math skills to find a match. (Use the metric table in your dictionary if you need help.) Write the letter on the right that represents your guess next to the numbered item on the left.

	Item		**Weight**
_____	1. average man	**a.**	36g
_____	2. coffee cup	**b.**	5kg
_____	3. six-pack of canned pop	**c.**	100kg
_____	4. liter of milk	**d.**	.5g
_____	5. full-grown house cat	**e.**	80kg
_____	6. large dog	**f.**	1kg
_____	7. medium-size car	**g.**	310g
_____	8. large orange	**h.**	2.5kg
_____	9. heavyweight boxer	**i.**	160g
_____	10. telephone (handset only)	**j.**	25kg
_____	11. transistor radio battery	**k.**	3¾ liter
_____	12. gallon of gas	**l.**	1600kg

11.5

Tracking the Miles

DIRECTIONS: Below is another kind of graph called a *bar graph*. (Earlier in this section you worked with a line graph.) The bar graph is another way of presenting data. This graph shows the number of miles run each week by six junior high track teams. Answer the question below and then make another bar graph from the data given.

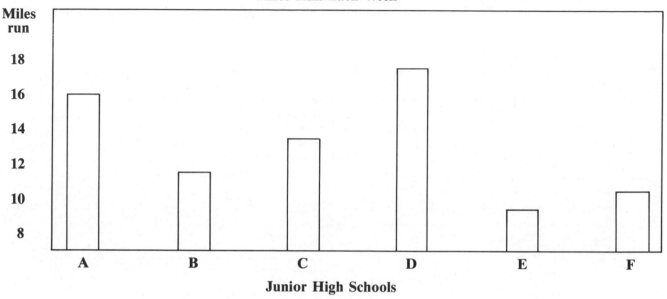

Miles Run Each Week

Junior High Schools

1. Which school ran the most miles each week? _____

2. Which school ran the least miles each week? _____

Now take the team "win" records listed here and make a record bar graph in the space below. Team A = 10, B = 6, C = 8, D = 13, E = 3, F = 4.

3. Do the data from both graphs show that the harder a team practices the more victories it will

probably win? _____

II.6

From *Mastermind.* Copyright © 1985 Scott, Foresman and Company.

COMPREHENSION   17

The Payment Plan

DIRECTIONS: Many people buy large household items such as washers or dryers by paying a set amount of money each month. This kind of purchasing is called "installment buying." The buyer (you) agrees to pay a set amount each month for a set number of months. This payment includes a fee (finance charge) that is a certain amount of money paid to the seller in addition to the item's cost. Therefore, the installment buying price is usually more (because of the finance charge) than just the cash price. See if you can calculate "cash" and "installment" prices in the chart below. The first item is worked for you. You'll need all your math skills to fill in the chart.

Item purchased	Cash price	Monthly Payment Plan			Finance charge	Difference between cash & installment price
		$ Per month	Number of months	Total		
EXAMPLE: Typewriter	$ 140	$ 7	24	$ 168	$ 28	$ 28
1. Stereo	250	10	30			
2. T.V.	390	24	20			
3. Table	190	11	20			
4. Clothes	180	17		204	24	
5. Chairs	220		18	270		50
6. Washer	285		10	330		
7. Dryer	220	10		220		
8. Moped	375	22	20	440		
9. Boat	1850					350
10. Car	4200		36			768

Complete this sentence: The difference between the _____ price and the _____ price

is the same as the _____ .

II.7

From *Mastermind*. Copyright © 1985 Scott, Foresman and Company.

Short and Sweet

DIRECTIONS: It is sometimes very helpful to put something you are trying to explain to a friend into different words. The new explanation may be the one he or she understands. See if you can rewrite the following statements in a different way, but make sure the same meaning is still there. (You might need a dictionary.) Can you shorten the statements? Write your sentences on the lines provided.

EXAMPLE: The man stretched the string tight and launched the pointed projectile toward the stationary object.

REWRITE: The man shot the arrow at the target.

1. The boy was told that he must cut down the green growth enclosed within the fence surrounding his own residence.

_____

_____

2. The light, brightly colored metal containers were taken from their holders, and their contents of primarily edible matter were consumed by the students at approximately 12:00 noon.

_____

_____

3. The girl peered intently at the printed pages of the bound volume.

_____

_____

4. The winged vehicle, lifted by its powerful engines, rose quickly from the hardened surface.

_____

_____

II.8

The Information Game

DIRECTIONS: When you comprehend something, you not only understand it but you can also pick out pieces of information. The following phrases tell *what, where, when, how,* or *who.*

Read the phrase and mark the proper box or boxes.

	What	Where	When	How	Who
1. the doctor					
2. Friday at the game					
3. door closed softly					
4. earlier that morning					
5. hurry to school					
6. say it faster					
7. across the state					
8. early Thanksgiving day					
9. over the barn					
10. my teacher					
11. maybe by tonight					
12. a caterpillar, crawling					
13. waves in the ocean					
14. the red firetruck					
15. the mailman					
16. at six o'clock					
17. very slowly					
18. the yellow cat					
19. today at school					
20. by coasting downhill					

II.9

Helpful Hints

The activities in this unit come under the category of "Applications." Application is "the ability to grasp the meaning of materials." You may be asked to use your math skills or to use information to solve problems.

The "Helpful Hints" section is designed to give you some suggestions and reminders before you begin the activities. We hope you'll find all the activities fun, but some are also meant to be hard and really make you think. That's why we put the "Helpful Hints" section first.

Take a few minutes to go through the following checklist. Read each hint. Then place a checkmark in the box to indicate that you understand the suggestions.

☐ **1.** Start with the first activity. Don't skip ahead.

☐ **2.** Application requires that you understand the theories, laws, and rules we are using. The best hint is to make sure you know which skill you're being asked to use. (EXAMPLES: compute, use the information, etc.) Underline the task we are asking you to perform (EXAMPLE: <u>make a graph</u>).

☐ **3.** Check *all* your calculations twice. Use scratch paper or a calculator if available.

☐ **4.** Some activities have examples. Look at them carefully.

☐ **5.** Have scratch paper handy. Use the scratch paper so you have plenty of room to see your own work.

☐ **6.** Keep a dictionary handy and look up any words you don't know.

☐ **7.** Ask a friend to look at your work if you get stuck.

☐ **8.** Ask your teacher to give you *one* specific hint. Try that hint before you ask for more help.

Season Average

DIRECTIONS: Graphs give us a good way to display information. Graphs help people see data and compare results. Look at the graph below and use the information on the graph to answer the questions. The graph shows the total points scored for the season by the Glendale Elementary School boys' fifth and sixth grade basketball team.

Season Point Totals

Number of points scored

```
100
 95
 90                                                          ____
 85              ____                                       |    |
 80             |    |      ____      ____                  |    |
 75             |    |     |    |    |    |                 |    |
 70   ____      |    |     |    |    |    |                 |    |
 65  |    |     |    |     |    |    |    |                 |    |
 60  |    |     |    |     |    |    |    |                 |    |
    Jimmie      Nick       Phil      Benji                  Dick
```

1. Which player scored the fewest points?

_____

2. Who scored the most points?

_____

3. What was the highest number of points scored? _____

4. What was the lowest number of points scored? _____

Application activities ask you to use skills you've already learned. Do you remember how to find averages? If you don't remember, get your math book and review.

5. What was the average score for the

team? _____

The team members also played in a Holiday Tournament. Make a graph showing the team scores for this tournament. Then figure the team's tournament average. Here are the team members' points: Benji 78, Jimmie 88, Phil 81, Dick 86, Nick 92.

6. What is the team's average at the

Holiday Tournament? _____

7. What is the difference between the regular season average and the tournament average?

_____

III.1

From *Mastermind.* Copyright © 1985 Scott, Foresman and Company.

Name _____

Measuring in Metric

DIRECTIONS: The following activity asks you to apply what you already know about measurement so you can solve the problems. You will need a ruler. Be sure the ruler has *metric* markings.

Using your ruler and your math skills, measure the length of the lines to the closest centimeter and figure the distance in centimeters around the shapes pictured. Show your work or use scratch paper. (If a measured distance is ½ cm or more, go to the next centimeter.) Write your answers in the blanks provided.

1.
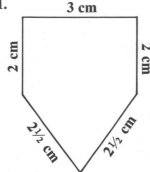

2.
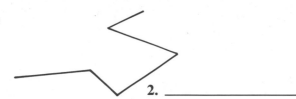

3.
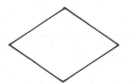

4.

5.
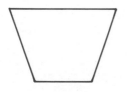

6.
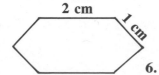

1. _____

2. _____

3. _____

4. _____

5. _____

6. _____

7.
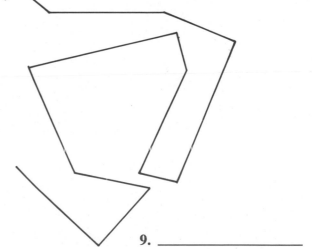

8.

9.
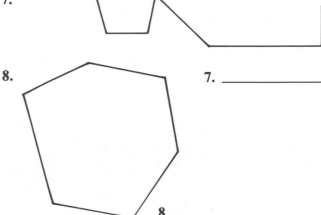

10.
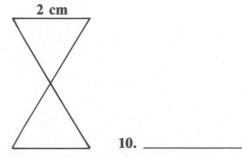

7. _____

8. _____

9. _____

10. _____

APPLICATIONS   23

Our Solar System

DIRECTIONS: Sometimes when you read something it will be necessary to remember the information and apply it somewhere else. The following paragraphs tell some details about the planets. Read each paragraph and then draw a diagram at the bottom of the page, showing how you apply the information you learned.

The planet that is closest to the sun is Mercury. It is about half as large as Earth and is the smallest planet. Venus is about 67 million miles from the sun; it looks brighter than a star.

Earth is, of course, the planet we live on. It is about 93 million miles from the sun. The Earth travels around the sun in 365 days. Mars is slightly smaller than Earth. It is located between Earth and the largest planet in our solar system, Jupiter.

Jupiter is the giant planet. It is so far from the sun that it is always cold. However, Uranus, Neptune, and Pluto are even farther away. Saturn is the second largest planet. It is also the planet with the rings around it; it is located between Jupiter and Uranus. Uranus takes 84 years to travel around the sun. It's almost as far away as Neptune.

Pluto is the farthest from the sun; it is bare and cold. Neptune takes 165 years to go around the sun; it has a diameter of almost 35,000 miles and is the next to the last planet from the sun.

Now, sketch the sun and the planets in their order.

III.3

Name _____

A Line of Pizzas

DIRECTIONS: The graph below is called a *line graph*. Like a bar graph, the line graph gives us information. Look at the graph below and find the information necessary to solve the problems or answer the questions that follow.

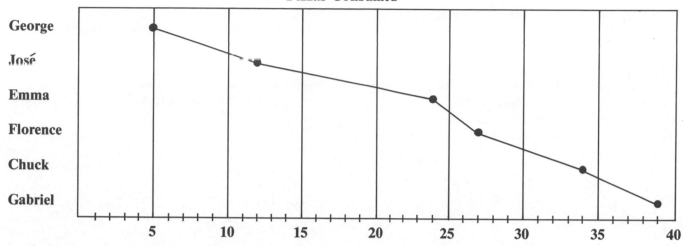

Pizzas Consumed

Who ate the fewest pizzas? _____

How many more pizzas did Emma eat than

José? _____

Using the idea of comparing by making a line graph, take the information listed here and make your own line graph. Use the box provided. This information tells how many home runs were hit by 5 different ball players: Tom = 6; Bob = 8; Ann = 10; Carl = 12; Sue = 14.

III.4

APPLICATIONS   25

Courtney's Day

DIRECTIONS: Figure out the answers to the problems that arose from Courtney's visit to the Video Arcade. You may need to write out equations to help find the answers. Use scratch paper so you have room to write.

1. Courtney had a $20 bill. If she went into the Video Arcade to get quarters, how many quarters did she get?

2. She played 6 games of Pac-Man, 12 games of Frogger, and received two free games. How much money did she have left? (Free games are *free*.)

3. The next games Courtney played took only dimes. She converted her money into dimes, except for $2.50 for lunch. How many dimes did she have?

4. Courtney met her brother, Dick, who insisted on having 7 quarters. After she parted with those, how much money did she have left?

5. On the way out of the Video Arcade, Courtney decided to deposit all the money she had left into a savings account, but first she bought a Garfield doll for $1.25. How much did she put into her account?

III.5

Chips Galore

DIRECTIONS: Answer the questions following each word problem. You may write out equations to help you. When you are finished, check your answers with ours.

A. Anne has 3 piles of plastic chips with 10 in each pile. Mary has 4 piles of chips with 8 in each pile. Elizabeth has 5 piles of chips with 5 in each pile.

1. Who has the most chips?

_____

2. Who has the fewest chips?

_____

3. How many chips does Anne have?

_____

4. How many chips does Mary have?

_____

5. How many chips does Elizabeth have?

_____

B. Chris has 4 piles of chips with 7 in each pile. Tim has 6 piles of chips with 5 in each pile. Joe has 8 piles of chips with 3 in each pile.

6. Who has the most chips?

_____

7. Who has the fewest chips?

_____

8. How many chips does Chris have?

_____

9. How many chips does Tim have?

_____

10. How many chips does Joe have?

_____

III.6

Growing Pains

DIRECTIONS: Answer the questions following each word problem. You may have to set up equations to figure out the correct answers.

John is 5 feet tall. His shadow is 3 inches shorter than he is at noon, but increases 1 inch per hour after noon.

1. How tall is John's shadow at

noon? _____

2. How tall is John's shadow at 4

PM? _____

3. How tall is John's shadow at 2

PM? _____

4. How tall is John's shadow at 8

PM? _____

Chris is 5 feet 1 inch tall. He is 10 years old. If he grows 1 inch every 6 months, how tall will he be:

5. at age 10½? _____

6. at age 12? _____

7. at age 14? _____

8. at age 9? _____

III.7

The Last Gallon

DIRECTIONS: The following problem requires you to think carefully about volume. Apply your knowledge of volume to solve the two sisters' dilemma in the story that follows.

One Gallon, No More!

Stacie and Kacie each have a jar. Stacie's jar holds 5 quarts of water and Kacie's jar holds 3 quarts of water. The girls' father asked them to go to the pump and get him exactly 1 gallon of water, no more!

The jars were not marked in any way. In 10 minutes the girls were back with the 1 gallon of water their father requested. How did the girls solve their problem of getting exactly 1 gallon, no more?

Write your solution here. Be specific. List each step in solving Stacie and Kacie's problem. Kacie and Stacie discovered two different solutions. See if you can find both solutions.

Stacie's Solution

Kacie's Solution

III.8

Analogies

DIRECTIONS: An analogy is a statement that points out a likeness, or a similarity. Some of the following analogies are not true. If the analogy is *true,* write T in the blank. If the analogy is *false,* decide which word is not correct and cross it out. Then write a word that will make it true.

EXAMPLES: *Correct:* Winter is to *summer* as *cold* is to *warm.*
Incorrect: Submarine is to *fish* as *kite* is to *dog. (Bird* is the correct answer.)

_____ 1. *Bicycle* is to *street* as *airplane* is to *ocean.*

_____ 2. *Clock* is to *time* as *thermometer* is to *distance.*

_____ 3. *Plate* is to *dishes* as *fork* is to *food.*

_____ 4. *Robin* is to *bird* as *collie* is to *dog.*

_____ 5. *Enormous* is to *huge* as *muddy* is to *unclear.*

_____ 6. *Low* is to *high* as *on* is to *in.*

_____ 7. *Glove* is to *ball* as *hook* is to *fish.*

_____ 8. *Rug* is to *wall* as *skin* is to *people.*

_____ 9. *Up* is to *down* as *in* is to *out.*

_____ 10. *Bashful* is to *bold* as *noisy* is to *loud.*

_____ 11. *Horse* is to *animal* as *apple* is to *fruit.*

_____ 12. *Car* is to *auto* as *canoe* is to *boat.*

Now that you've discovered how much fun analogies are, write 5 analogies of your own!

III.9

ANALYSIS

Helpful Hints

These activities are from the category called "Analysis." Analysis is "the ability to break down material into its various parts." You might be asked to construct graphs or charts or to solve math problems.

Take some time to read over the hints we've listed below before you attempt the activities. These suggestions will give you some specific things to think about as you tackle this unit. The activities are fun, but you can slip up if you're not careful.

Read each hint and place a checkmark in the box if you understand the suggestion. This will help show that you understand what you're being asked to do.

☐ **1.** Start with activity 1; don't jump ahead.

☐ **2.** Have your scratch paper handy. Be sure to give yourself plenty of room so you can follow your own work.

☐ **3.** Reread the definition of *Analysis* at the top of this page. Be sure you know the kinds of things you'll be asked to do.

☐ **4.** In the directions of the activity, underline the skill you're asked to use.
Example: <u>Construct</u> a graph like ours.

☐ **5.** Look at the whole activity. If you see any words or terms you don't know, look them up in your dictionary before you begin working.

☐ **6.** Some activities have examples. Study them carefully for help in completing the activity.

☐ **7.** Look for the hints that might be in the directions, such as *identify* the differences.

☐ **8.** If it's OK with your teacher, ask a friend for his or her ideas if you get stuck. Sometimes another student can see something you've missed.

☐ **9.** See if your teacher can help you. But be sure to ask your teacher a specific question. Do not say, "I'm stuck, can you help?" Think about your question before you go to your teacher.

☐ **10.** If you're really stuck, *stop*. Put your book away and come back to it later. Remember, some problems are harder than others!

Shaping Up

DIRECTIONS: Read the directions below and follow the instructions for each problem. If you complete each problem correctly, you should be able to put together the final figure.

On a separate piece of paper, draw the shapes requested from the information given. You'll need to know some *math terms*, and you'll need a ruler and a compass. If you don't know a term, look it up in the dictionary.

1. Draw a rectangle that has 4 sides. Each side should be exactly 1 inch long. What is the name

of this kind of rectangle? _____

2. Make a triangle with a *base* 2 inches long and the other two sides 1½ inches long.

3. Make a circle with a *radius* of ½ inch.

4. Draw a rectangle that has two sides *parallel* to each other that arc ¾ inch long and two sides *parallel* to each other that are 1½ inches long.

5. Draw a circle with a *diameter* of 1 inch.

6. Now put this together:

   a. Draw a line that is 1½ times (×) the length of the *base* of your triangle.

   b. Draw a *perpendicular line* going up on each end of your base line that is the same length as one of the *small sides* of your second rectangle.

   c. *Connect* those two lines to form a rectangle.

   d. Place a circle on the left side of your rectangle that has a *radius* the same as that of the first circle you made. Place the circle so its center is located at the bottom corner of your rectangle.

   e. Place another circle on the right side of your rectangle. Make this circle have a *diameter* equal to the one in the *second circle* you made. Place the circle so its middle is located at the bottom-right corner of your rectangle.

   f. Now draw a line directly out from the right side of your rectangle. Make this line equal to the distance of one of the lengths of the *two equal* sides of your triangle.

IV.1

Grouping the Groups

DIRECTIONS: Organize the following words so that they are grouped together. You must supply a main title, and then you must organize the list words into one or more subgroups. (EXAMPLE: net, Football, hoop, kicking tee, Basketball, helmet)

Sports:

A. Basketball
   1. net
   2. hoop

B. Football
   1. kicking tee
   2. helmet

1. glove
   catcher
   positions
   baseball
   bat

   pitcher
   outfielders
   ball
   equipment
   infielders

2. apple
   rice
   Meat Group
   milk
   macaroni
   ice cream
   Grain Group
   bean
   pork
   Milk Group
   beef

   fish
   yogurt
   Fruit and Vegetable Group
   bread
   lettuce
   chicken
   cheese
   cereal
   Four Food Groups
   orange

IV.2

ANALYSIS   33

The Hidden Shape

DIRECTIONS: Look carefully at the pictures below and then answer the questions that follow.

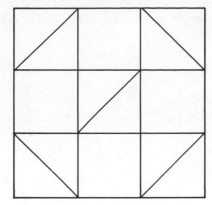

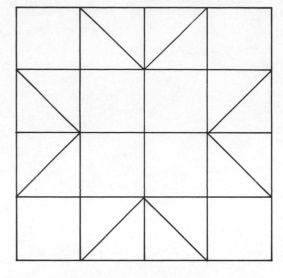

1. How many squares are there that have

nothing inside them at all?_____

2. How many triangles are there?_____

3. How many squares are there that have

nothing inside them at all?_____

4. How many triangles are there?_____

5. Now draw a large square that has 5 squares with nothing inside them and 8 triangles. Use a separate piece of paper.

IV.3

Food for Thought

DIRECTIONS: You need food in a variety of forms to give your body the energy you need to do the things you want to do. The United States Department of Agriculture has identified four basic food groups that will supply us with all the essential nutrients we need. The four groups are: (1) milk and milk products; (2) meat, fish, eggs, and nuts; (3) vegetables and fruits; (4) cereal products.

Each day our diet should include proper amounts from each group. Look at the chart below and identify what group is missing from the *daily* diets listed. You'll have to decide what group the foods fit into to determine what's missing for the day.

Name	Breakfast	Lunch	Dinner	Missing
EXAMPLE	cereal, milk, juice	vegetable soup, crackers, pop	salad, green beans, milk, fruit cup, bread	meat group
Sue	toast, orange juice	hamburger and french fries, soda pop	fish, peas, fruit cocktail, bread, ice tea	
Bill	coffee	cottage cheese, ice tea	salad, coffee	
Jan	milk, bacon and eggs, toast, juice	chocolate cake, hot tea	bacon sandwich, milk	
Kacie	juice, donut	salad, ice tea	cottage cheese, tomatoes, cucumbers, ice cream	
Clark	milk, toast	hot dog, soda pop	beef steak, bread, cottage cheese, coffee	
Dick	eggs, sausage, coffee	ham sandwich, coffee	fish, bread, ice tea	

Now, list a diet for yourself for a day. You must have all four groups in *each meal*.

Name	Breakfast	Lunch	Dinner

IV.4

The Big Picture

DIRECTIONS: Let's look at our solar system. Select a current encyclopedia yearbook or a book on astronomy that shows you the solar system. Use your *reference book* to draw the solar system according to our directions. In the space provided, draw a 1″-diameter circle on the right side of the square to represent the sun. Place the nine planets of our solar system in order, moving in a *straight line* from right to left. (You can guess at the distance and size for this activity.) Color the Earth *green* and all the planets larger than the Earth *blue*. Color all planets smaller than the Earth *red*.

Now answer these questions.

1. How many planets are larger than the Earth?

_____

2. How many planets are smaller than the

Earth? _____

3. What's the second farthest planet away from

the Earth? _____

4. What's the second farthest planet away from

the Sun? _____

5. What planet has the most moons?

_____

How many? _____

IV.5

Word Power

DIRECTIONS: Let's check your vocabulary again, by looking at the *relationship* between words. You can show a different *level* of meaning by using a different word to make your sentence stronger.

Complete the lists below by selecting two words from the word box that best fit the blanks. You might need your dictionary to help with some words.

		Stronger Meaning	**Strongest Meaning**
EXAMPLE:	pretty	lovely	beautiful
1.	encourage	_____	_____
2.	remove	_____	_____
3.	oppose	_____	_____
4.	ponder	_____	_____
5.	daze	_____	_____
6.	singe	_____	_____
7.	pry	_____	_____
8.	inflame	_____	_____
9.	lift	_____	_____

Word Box

resist	paralyze	enrage
weigh	hinder	stun
eradicate	infuriate	sear
meddle	char	heave
hoist	stimulate	deliberate
exterminate	intrude	inspire

IV.6

Antonyms, Synonyms, or Homonyms

DIRECTIONS: Do you know the difference between an antonym, a synonym, and a homonym? This problem requires that you do. If you don't know what the words mean, look them up. The activity below requires that you decide which word pairs are antonyms, synonyms, or homonyms.

Here is a list of paired words. After each pair indicate whether the words are antonyms (a), synonyms (s), or homonyms (h).

Paired Words   **Your Answer**

1. hire—higher _____

2. profit—prophet _____

3. thin—flimsy _____

4. need—knead _____

5. serial—cereal _____

6. maize—maze _____

7. mane—main _____

8. lax—lacks _____

9. dark—light _____

10. weather—whether _____

11. here—hear _____

12. boy—girl _____

13. pare—pair _____

14. moist—wet _____

15. isle—aisle _____

16. pretty—lovely _____

17. comical—funny _____

18. high—low _____

19. slow—fast _____

20. jovial—happy _____

Following the Numbers

DIRECTIONS: Sometimes a few short sentences can be very confusing unless they are read very carefully. We've written two short paragraphs for you. Read each one carefully. Then answer the questions that follow each paragraph. See if you can figure out the answers in your head. Write your answers in the spaces provided.

Terrance will be 12 years old tomorrow. Terrill is 3 years older than Tad. Tad is 9 years old. Tommy is 6 years younger than Terrance. Thomas is 1 year older than Terrill.

1. How old is the oldest student?

_____

2. How old is the youngest student?

_____

3. How much older than Tommy is Terrill?

_____

4. How old was Thomas 3 years ago?

_____

5. How much older than Terrance is Thomas?

_____

6. When will Terrance and Terrill first be the *same* age? How old will they be?

_____

Kacie has 12 stamps. She gives 3 of them to Tracy. She is given 4 more by Jerri. She now has 20 stamps less than Stacie.

7. How many stamps does Kacie have?

_____

8. How many stamps does Stacie have?

_____

9. How many stamps do Kacie and Stacie have together?_____

IV.8

Double Meaning

DIRECTIONS: Analyzing material sometimes includes analyzing the relationship between parts. When we analyze some words, we see that they would make sense in more than one way.

Look at the two definitions. Then choose the *one word* that satisfies *both* definitions.

1. name of a flower
    colored part of the eye   lily   tulip   iris

2. what's left after a fire
    name of a tree   poplar   ash   elm

3. the way you feel
    you may have to pay it   well   okay   fine

4. carpenter uses
    found on fingers   boards   nails   saw

5. a part of the body
    a piece of furniture   chairs   chest   table

6. not warm
    an illness   chilly   cold   draft

7. growing and green
    a manufacturing place   factory   machine   plant

8. a vegetable on a vine
    to mash something flat   crush   smash   squash

9. a tool to cut wood
    looked and noticed   ax   saw   hatchet

10. something used to measure
    someone who runs a country   president   ruler   queen

IV.9

SYNTHESIS

Helpful Hints

The activities in this unit belong to the "Synthesis" category. Synthesis is "the ability to put different parts together to form a new whole." You may be asked to rearrange, group, or organize.

Before you begin the Synthesis unit, take time to go over the hints and reminders listed below. Remember, some activities are harder than others, so don't be afraid to come back and review these suggestions and hints. The "Helpful Hints" section will help you get started and give you hints if you get stuck.

Read each hint and place a checkmark in the box provided. This will show your teacher that you understand the suggestions.

☐ **1.** Start with the first activity. Don't jump ahead. Do the activities in the order presented.

☐ **2.** Remember, the "Synthesis" unit requires that you understand how the different parts fit together to form a whole. Be sure you know the skills you are being asked to use. (EXAMPLE: Arrange the squares to form a new object.)

☐ **3.** Have some scratch paper, scissors, and a ruler (one that uses metric) ready to use.

☐ **4.** Look carefully at any examples provided. Try to understand the solutions.

☐ **5.** Write down everything you know about the problem. Be sure to write down what you're asked to do.

☐ **6.** Ask a friend for *one* hint.

☐ **7.** If you don't get the right answer, put the problem away for awhile, and then come back to it later.

☐ **8.** Ask your teacher for *one* specific hint. Try that one hint before you ask for another.

A Metric Drawing

DIRECTIONS: Here is a ruler that is 1 decimeter long. (One decimeter = 10 centimeters.) Trace the ruler, mount it on cardboard, and follow the directions.

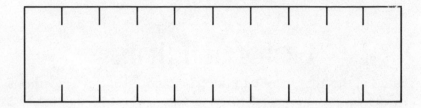

1. Label all the lines you draw!
2. Draw a 1-decimeter line straight up and down on a piece of paper.
3. Starting at each end of this line, draw a 5-centimeter line to the right.
4. Then draw a 5-centimeter line straight up from the open end of both these lines.

5. At the end of these two lines, draw two 5-centimeter lines to the right.
6. Join the ends of these two lines with a 1-decimeter line.

V.1

The Paper Game

DIRECTIONS: Here are 10 squares numbered 1 through 10. Follow the instructions for each problem as closely as possible. (You might want to cut some squares out of paper to help you solve these problems.)

| 1 | 2 | 3 | 4 | 5 | 6 | 7 | 8 | 9 | 10 |

1. Using squares like the ones above, arrange them to make a capital T. All the even-numbered squares must be vertical and all the odd-numbered squares must be horizontal.

2. Now make a capital S with your squares. All the even numbers must be on the up-down line and all the odd numbers must be on the across axes.

V.2

The Secret Message

DIRECTIONS: The message below is written in secret code. Each number represents a single letter of the alphabet. Study the code and then decode the secret message.

A = 1, B = 4, C = 7, D = 11, E = 14, F = 17, G = 21, H = 24, I = 27, J = 32, K = 36, L = 40, M = 45, N = 49, O = 53, P = 58, Q = 62, R = 66, S = 72, T = 77, U = 82, V = 88, W = 93, X = 98, Y = 104, Z = 109.

1 / 21,53,53,11 / 11,14,7,53,11,14,66 / 1,40,93,1,104,72 / 40,53,53,36,72 / 17,53,66 / 1 / 72,104,72,77,14,45 . 7,1,49 / 104,53,82 / 17,27,21,82,66,14 / 53,82,77 / 53,82,66 / 72,104,72,77,14,45 ? / 104,53,82,66 / 1,49,72,93,14,66,72 / 77,53 / 77,24,14 / 62,82,14,72,77,27,53,49,72 / 4,14,40,53,93 / 93,27,40,40 / 77,14,40,40 / 82,72 / 27,17 / 104,53,82 / 17,27,21,82,66,14,11 / 53,82,77 / 53,82,66 / 72,104,72,77,14,45 . 53,36,1,104 / 72,24,14,66,40,53,7,36 , 21,53,53,11 / 40,82,7,36 !

Here are some questions about our coding system. To answer these you may want to list the entire alphabet on a sheet of paper with the corresponding numbers. After listing the alphabet, look for a pattern in the code. The pattern involves the difference between the numbers. Look carefully before you answer the questions below.

1. How many times were the differences in the amount between consecutive numbers in the code changed? _____

2. What is the greatest difference between two consecutive numbers? _____

3. The value between letters changed in a designed pattern. When did the difference between consecutive numbers increase by one additional point? _____

Everything in Its Place

DIRECTIONS: A very important scientific skill is the skill of classifying. *Classifying* means putting things into categories. Take a close look at the items in the list below. Then place each under a category it best fits. Place the letter and the word in the column. Items may fit into more than one category.

a. insects	**e.** grass	**i.** pencils	**m.** teachers	**q.** food
b. snakes	**f.** sheep	**j.** water	**n.** principals	**r.** house
c. a rose	**g.** birds	**k.** paper	**o.** oxygen	**s.** bike
d. table	**h.** children	**l.** clothes	**p.** ants	**t.** teeth

Keep in mind that items placed under a heading represent something that goes with that heading, or might best belong there, or that might be used by its heading (that is, humans, animals, and plants all use or need water).

EXAMPLE:

Human beings	Animals	Man-made things	Plants
m. teachers			

V.4

The Parts Add Up

DIRECTIONS: A good thinking skill is the ability to see how numbers can be arranged to form new whole numbers. Arrange the numbers 1–10 in the pyramid picture so that the top line adds up to 3, the second line adds up to 15, the third to 15, and the fourth to 22.

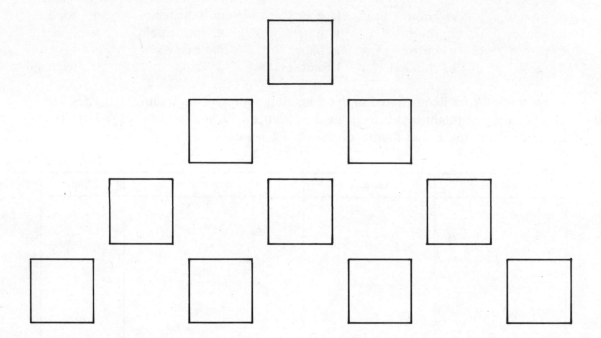

The Big T

DIRECTIONS: The picture below in the first box is a capital T. The T as you see it in Box 1 is the result of putting together the four different parts found in Box 2. Sometimes puzzles like this are called "optical illusions," because they appear to be different than they really are. Take a piece of white paper and trace over the parts in Box 2. Carefully cut out the parts with scissors and see if you can rearrange the parts to create the T as shown in Box 1. When you think you have it right, rearrange the parts in Box 3. Remember, your T must look exactly like the T in Box 1.

Box 1   The T

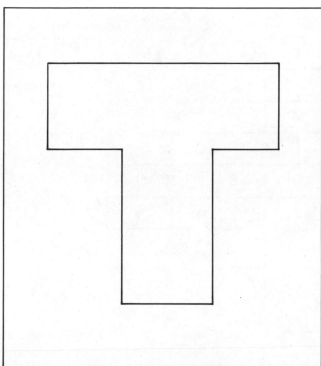

Box 2   The Parts

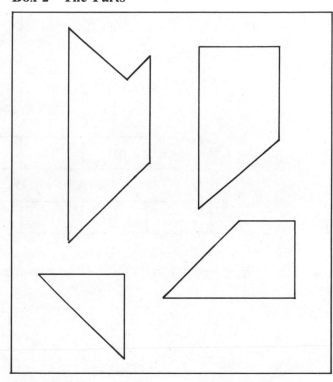

Box 3   Arrange your solution here:

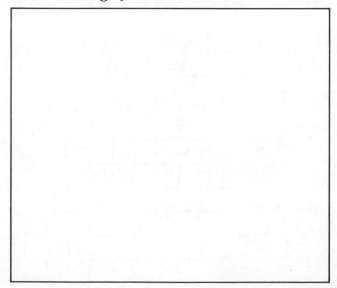

V.6

Mountain Building

DIRECTIONS: Synthesis means "to put the parts together." You will now have a chance to build a "word wall"—but the wall looks more like a mountain! You will start with only one letter in the top brick. By filling each box with a letter you will end up with a new word in each row, until you finally make a 7-letter word in the bottom row. You must use at least 1 letter from the row above each of your words, and you must add at least 1 new letter to each row. (Look carefully at our sample.)

Sample mountain:

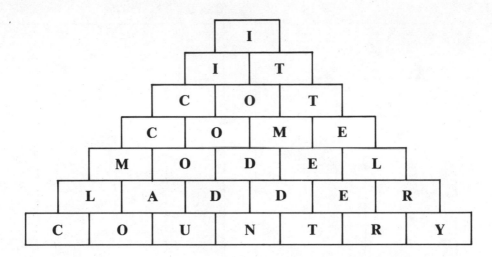

Now make 3 mountains of your own:

V·7

Mystery Dots

DIRECTIONS: There are nine dots in the work space below. Look very carefully at the nine dots. They are equally spaced. Now that you've looked carefully at the dots, see if you can *connect* all nine dots with four straight lines. *Do not* take your pencil off the paper. You *may not retrace any line* before beginning the next. All four lines must be connected one following the other. The lines may cross one another if necessary.

Well, does it sound difficult? Give it a try. Good Luck!

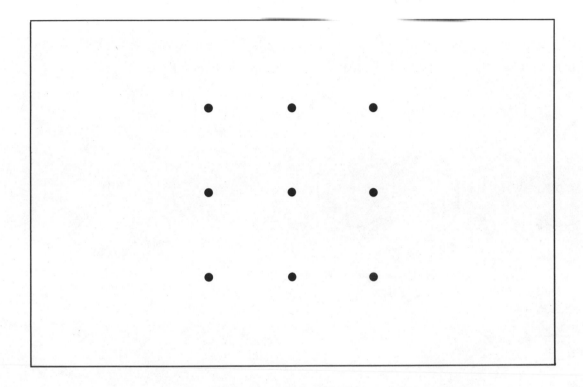

When you connected your dots, what shape did your four lines make? _____

V.8

The Clue's the Thing

DIRECTIONS: Each center circle below has a series of words attached to it. Each word is a *clue* to help you determine what the center represents. Read the clues attached to each center circle. Then write your answer in the center circle.

1.

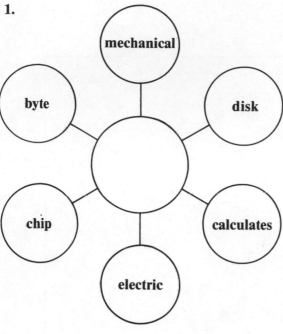

2.

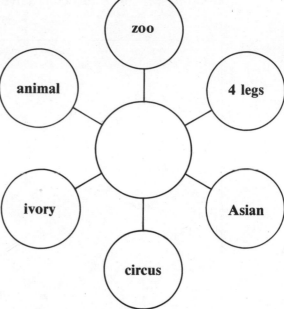

3.

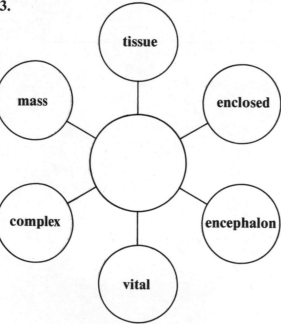

4.

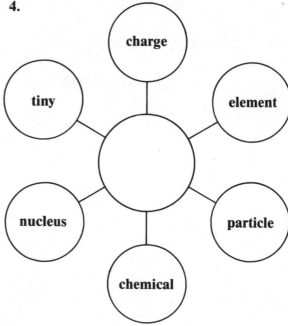

V.9

EVALUATION VI

Helpful Hints

The activities in this unit are from the "Evaluation" category. Evaluation is "the ability to judge the value of materials being used."

Evaluation activities are usually the most difficult and usually involve the most thinking skills and processes. The hints for this unit are also designed to make you think. Read each suggestion and place a checkmark in the box, indicating you understand what we've suggested.

Your teacher will correct all the activities in this section. Since you will be asked to *judge* or *decide,* all your answers will be correct, but only if you provide support for your solutions.

☐ **1.** Read the directions and be sure to underline what you're being asked to do. (make judgments , compose , and so on.)

☐ **2.** Be sure you have a dictionary handy. Defining terms and words you don't know will help you find your solution.

☐ **3.** Write down a list of the details you were able to find in the introductory material. Go back over the introduction to make sure you've found all the details.

☐ **4.** Look at the examples and make sure you understand them before you try the whole activity.

☐ **5.** Ask a friend to review your work to see whether he or she can give you a hint.

☐ **6.** Ask your teacher to give *one* specific hint.

☐ **7.** If you still can't get an answer, ask your teacher for a second specific hint.

☐ **8.** If you're still stuck, don't go on. Review this checklist and review what you know about the problem.

☐ **9.** Remember, there are no right or wrong answers.

☐ **10.** Be sure you list the reasons why you made the decisions you made.

Finding Meaning in Proverbs

DIRECTIONS: One meaning of evaluation is "to explain or describe." A proverb is a short saying that has been used to teach a lesson. *For example,* the proverb "Great oaks from little acorns grow," may mean to you that each little person has a chance to grow up to be a great person.

Listed below are twelve common proverbs. On a separate sheet of paper tell in your own words what the proverbs mean. Then write, in a few sentences, why you think you have found the correct meaning.

1. Don't bite the hand that feeds you.
2. Take the bull by the horns.
3. Don't let the grass grow under your feet.
4. Actions speak louder than words.
5. All that glitters is not gold.
6. You can't teach an old dog new tricks.

7. It's an ill wind that blows no good.
8. A man is known by the company he keeps.
9. Barking dogs seldom bite.
10. Do not put off until tomorrow what you can do today.
11. Necessity is the mother of invention.
12. Birds of a feather flock together.

VI.1

The Visitor

DIRECTIONS: Here is a fictional story about what might happen if *Extra Terrestrials* (E.T.s) really visited Earth. Read the story and answer the questions. Then on a separate sheet of paper write at least two reasons to support each of your answers.

Like so many visitors in the past, Poltic eased his silent intergalactic flying laboratory into the usual place in the deserted valley in the desert. Poltic was to be the last researcher to the planet Earth. The next arrivals from Democraton would be the official ambassadors, who would bring the open offerings of friendship, based on Poltic's findings.

Poltic, as the last of the researchers, was to be responsible for gathering the final data on how the humans of Earth live with each other. In his disguise as a human being, he would drive to a nearby city and study first-hand how humans live together. His disguise (including his clothes, language, and even his car) was created by a Democraton scientist who used the data from the last secret visit to Earth that took place twenty-five years ago.

Answer each question *yes* or *no*. Then on a separate sheet of paper, list at least 2 reasons for each answer you gave.

1. Do you think the visitors from Democraton will be peaceful? _____

2. Did the Democratons think it was important to know something about Earthlings before they made contact? _____

3. It appears that the Democratons do not want to be noticed until they are prepared.

_____

4. Poltic may have some difficulty going unnoticed in an Earth city.

_____

5. Poltic will close the final chapter of Phase I of the visitors' plans. _____

6. The Democratons appear to be concerned with gathering knowledge.

VI.2

Passing Judgment

DIRECTIONS: When you evaluate something, you judge the value of it. Thus, there is no "right" or "wrong" answer, as long as you have a good reason to support (or prove) your answer.

Decide whether each of the following ten statements is true or false. On a separate sheet of paper mark each statement T for *true* or F for *false* and then give a reason for your answer. Try to give an *example* that supports your judgment.

1. All rich people are dishonest.

2. A dictionary is better than a thesaurus.

3. A person who does not read a lot is not well informed.

4. The smartest boy in our class is puny; therefore, all smart kids are poor athletes.

5. X is to Y as Y is to Z, so Y has the same relationship to X as it does to Z.

6. The sun is shining, so we know it cannot possibly rain today.

7. C is larger than A but smaller than B; therefore, A is smaller than either B or C.

8. One of the astronauts was left-handed; most scientific experts are left-handed.

9. It was foggy this morning; we won't be able to see the horizon all day long.

10. The winner of the race was riding a 5-speed bike; that proves that 5-speeds are the best.

VI.3

Believe It or Not

DIRECTIONS: Sometimes when we read, we will need to decide whether we are reading fact or opinion. A *fact*, as you know, is something that you can prove and support with reasons. An *opinion*, on the other hand, is how you feel about something.

Decide whether the following statements are fact or opinion. Write an F in the blank for fact; an O in the blank for opinion. Then on a separate sheet of paper, list the reasons for each of your answers.

_____ **1.** The man was lying in bed but was not asleep.

_____ **2.** The lights on the Christmas tree were beautiful.

_____ **3.** The trainer of the dolphin at Sea World was very patient.

_____ **4.** The winning score came with 10 seconds left to play.

_____ **5.** Strawberry ice cream tastes better than chocolate.

_____ **6.** The Smiths have the best garden in town.

_____ **7.** Every seat on the school bus was full.

_____ **8.** The tourist town was the friendliest in the West.

_____ **9.** The plane was running 7 minutes behind schedule.

_____ **10.** Corn is the best-tasting vegetable available in summer.

_____ **11.** In the final league standings, Mike was the poorest batter.

_____ **12.** Every school library should have carpeting on the floor.

_____ **13.** The new Raiders' stadium was filled to capacity with fans.

_____ **14.** The gifts look very fascinating.

VI.4

Two Sides

DIRECTIONS: Good evaluation skills require that both sides of any situation be considered before a conclusion is drawn. Read carefully the fictitious situation presented below. Then answer the questions and follow the specific directions.

The Cure

A brilliant scientist develops a drug for a fatal disease that had previously been incurable. This cure is the only one in the whole world. The scientist begins manufacturing the miracle drug and selling it for a large sum of money. She makes a great fortune manufacturing and selling this drug.

A man of very modest means who's wife has the fatal disease finds out that a cure is available, but he can't afford the drug. He tries everything he can think of to raise money, but he can't get enough. The man asks the scientist to reduce the cost, but she says she can't do that or everyone would ask for such help and she wouldn't make the money the drug is worth.

The man, in desperation, steals the drug and gives it to his wife. He is caught and arrested for the crime of stealing. He is put in jail, convicted of the crime of stealing, and brought before the judge for sentencing.

You're the judge. Answer the yes or no questions below. Then, on a separate sheet of paper, list why you gave your answer (pros) and also what you think the reasons would be for the opposite answer (cons). Divide your paper in half, Pros on one side and Cons on the other. This is called listing the pros and cons of a situation. Remember, the pros support your answers and the cons the opposing answer.

1. Do you think the man was guilty of a

crime? _____ (List the pros and cons.)

2. Should the scientist be allowed to make

money that way? _____ (List the pros and cons.)

3. Should the man be put in jail for what

he did? _____ (List the pros and cons.)

4. Do you think the scientist is guilty of a

crime? _____ (List the pros and cons.)

5. Should laws ever be changed to keep someone out of jail or to put someone in

jail?_____ (List the pros and cons.)

VI.5

The Planet Zeb

DIRECTIONS: Read the following paragraph very carefully. You may want to take a few notes because the questions that follow are based on the paragraph. The questions ask you to make judgments about the conclusions listed. All the conclusions are based on the information found in the paragraph. Think carefully before you respond. (Use your dictionary to look up any words you do not know.) *Remember,* your answers are as good as ours, but be sure you have a *reason* for your answer.

Aliens

On the distant planet Zeb, in another galaxy, live two groups of people. The Clingons live in the dark, damp, hot underground portion of the planet, while the Photons live in the warm, bright, green, comfortable, above-ground climate. The Photons are interested in the environment, are concerned about all living things, and always try to live in harmony with others. On the other hand, the Clingons abuse the environment and do what they want without thinking about others. The Photons help the Clingons when they have troubles, and never ask to be paid for their help. The Clingons are friendly but never volunteer their services. The Photons make rules for everyone. The Clingons have few rules and do not really follow the rules of others. The Photons and Clingons live together without any major difficulties primarily because the Photons work at keeping the peace.

On a separate sheet of paper, write *yes* if you agree with the statement and *no* if you disagree with it. After each answer tell why you agree (yes) or disagree (no).

1. The Clingons are friendly people.
2. The Photons would make good neighbors.
3. The Clingons care about the quality of others' lives.
4. The Clingons are concerned only about themselves.
5. The Photons organize their world in a fair way.
6. The Clingons probably have messy cities.

7. The Clingons are probably responsible for keeping the planet Zeb peaceful.
8. It appears that two groups of people who think differently can live together on the planet Zeb.
9. It would be difficult for the Clingons to live on the planet Earth.
10. I believe the Photons would be good friends to the people of Earth.

VI.6

Feelings

DIRECTIONS: The English language has many words and combinations of words and phrases that describe people, animals, things, events, and even places, by giving us a "feeling" about them. Listed below are some words and combinations of words and phrases that give some "feelings." Some words make us think about "good things" and some words make us think about "bad things," or at least things that don't make us feel good. Look at the list below. Place a + in the *evaluation space* for those words you "feel good" about, and a − for those words that "don't" make you feel good. After you've made your decisions, write a complete sentence in the space provided, using the word to show how it made you feel (+ or −). You can't be wrong. (You can use a dictionary if you don't know the word.) If you really don't have a feeling, write a 0, but you must still use the word in a sentence.

EXAMPLE: pretty smile   __+__
　　　　　Her pretty smile made everyone feel good.

Words　　　　　　　　　　　**Evaluation**

1. Soft and cuddly   _____

2. Lovable   _____

3. Sharp and jagged   _____

4. Evil eye   _____

5. Decent, kind, caring   _____

6. Considerate and helpful   _____

7. Bland   _____

8. Teary eyed   _____

9. Gentle and warm   _____

10. Dumpy and messy   _____

VI.7

In a Galaxy Far, Far Away

DIRECTIONS: This evaluation problem asks you to make some *judgments based on* the *information* found in the following story. After you've read the story, follow the directions.

The Story of Hans Lee

Hans Lee, after much hard work and study, became the Star Fleet's youngest captain. He was responsible for keeping peace in the North Quarter of the galaxy. He used his skills, knowledge, and training to help other galaxy members solve their disagreements. He spent most of his working hours studying about and listening to others. He encouraged those who disagreed to talk together and to work out their problems. His starship was not equipped with any weapons. His concerned, quiet approach made him well liked by others, and aliens of every type and age came to Hans Lee for advice. There was never a serious problem in the North Quarter. His many achievements soon made him the most decorated 17-year-old in the Star Fleet command.

Do you think *you* would like Hans Lee? Find out by answering these questions:

1. Why do you think Hans Lee was probably a good student? (List at least 2 reasons.)

_____

_____

_____

_____

2. Why would you want Hans Lee to help you settle a disagreement? (List 2 reasons.)

_____

_____

_____

3. What do you think were Hans Lee's best qualities? (List at least 3 reasons.)

_____

_____

_____

_____

4. Why do you think others liked Hans Lee? (List at least 2 reasons.)

_____

_____

_____

5. On a separate sheet of paper, write your own short story showing what you believe might happen to Hans Lee as he grows older.

VI.8

Your Judgment Please

DIRECTIONS: We told you that the evaluation activities would probably ask you to make comparisons and judge answers from the information given. This activity involves a special kind of comparison known as an *analogy*. An analogy is a statement that points out a likeness, or a similarity. An example of an analogy is: *Manager* is to *store* as *captain* is to _____ . (Did you guess ship or plane? If you did, you are right!) We want you to judge our analogies. Tell us whether you agree or disagree with them. Then, in a sentence or two, tell why you agree or disagree. Write an A if you agree with our analogy, a D if you disagree.

EXAMPLE: *FLEECE* is to *sheep* as *paint* is to *house*.   __A__

REASON: Fleece is on the outside of a sheep and paint is on the outside of a house.

1. Analogy: *ARTIST* is to *picture* as *writer* is to *book*.   _____

   Reason: _____

   _____

2. Analogy: *NET* is to *fish* as *trap* is to *bear*.   _____

   Reason: _____

   _____

3. Analogy: *LAUGH* is to *humor* as *shiver* is to *feet*.   _____

   Reason: _____

   _____

4. Analogy: *TELEVISION* is to *entertainment* as *jogging* is to *exercise*.   _____

   Reason: _____

   _____

5. Analogy: *SANDPAPER* is to *rough* as *pillow* is to *soft*.   _____

   Reason: _____

   _____

6. Analogy: *PEN* is to *ink* as *typewriter* is to *ribbon*.   _____

   Reason: _____

   _____

7. Analogy: *BRUSH* is to *teeth* as *polish* is to *shoes*.   _____

   Reason: _____

   _____

8. Analogy: *FILTH* is to *disease* as *speeding* is to *accident*.   _____

   Reason: _____

   _____

VI.9

ANSWER KEY

I.1 (1 point per correct answer); total points: 14
1. g — beet
2. k — celery
3. m — peas
4. n — spinach
5. c — cucumber
6. e — carrot
7. h — radish
8. b — lettuce
9. i — corn
10. a — tomato
11. j — cabbage
12. l — onion
13. f — string bean
14. d — potato

I.2 (1 point per correct answer); total points: 38; extra credit: 7
1. Did Standard Proofreading Practices
2. Iowa
3. East Coast, Super Suds
4. When, San Francisco, Bowens Company, Jim Johnson
5. National Education Association, N.E.A., American Federation Teachers, A.F.T.
6. Midlands Mall Shopping Center
7. Colonel
8. Latin
9. Three, Mernard
10. The, Vermont
11. The bat boy raced to pick up the dropped hat.
12. The new teacher asked for the students to raise their hands if they had any questions.

I.3 (1 point per correct answer); total points: 12

I.4 (1 point per correct answer); total points: 15
1. furniture
2. table
3. sink
4. couch
5. chairs
6. lamp
7. television
8. garden
9. lawn
10. picnic table
11. mother
12. sister
13. brother
14. father
15. housekeeper

I.5 (2 points per correct answer); total points: 24
1. c
2. b
3. c
4. d
5. d
6. d
7. a
8. c
9. b
10. b
11. a
12. b

I.6 (1 point per correct answer); total points: 17

I.7 (1 point per correct answer); total points: 20
1. custodian
2. principal
3. teachers
4. students
5. math
6. writing
7. gym
8. spelling
9. reading
10. bell
11. desk
12. pencil
13. pen
14. paper
15. books
16. school
17. chair
18. clocks
19. lunch
20. recess

I.8 (2 points per correct answer); total points: 30
1. c
2. i
3. b
4. m
5. o
6. e
7. g
8. f
9. j
10. k
11. h
12. d
13. l
14. a
15. n

I.9 (1 point per correct answer); total points: 24
1. sale, sail
2. waste, waist
3. meet, meat
4. sore, soar
5. flee, flea
6. steel, steal
7. meet, part
8. own, rent
9. end, start
10. slow, fast
11. busy, idle
12. owe, pay

II.1 (1 point per correct answer); total points: 65
1. 20 = 2 × 10, 20 × 1, 4 × 5
2. 6 = 2 × 3, 6 × 1
3. 12 = 3 × 4, 2 × 6, 12 × 1
4. 33 = 11 × 3, 33 × 1
5. 21 = 7 × 3, 21 × 1
6. 24 = 6 × 4, 3 × 8, 12 × 2, 24 × 1
7. 25 = 5 × 5, 25 × 1
8. 36 = 6 × 6, 12 × 3, 36 × 1, 4 × 9, 18 × 2
9. 40 = 5 × 8, 2 × 20, 4 × 10, 40 × 1
10. 60 = 3 × 20, 6 × 10, 12 × 5, 60 × 1, 30 × 2, 15 × 4
11. 45 = 9 × 5, 15 × 3, 45 × 1
12. 50 = 25 × 2, 10 × 5, 50 × 1
13. 90 = 30 × 3, 45 × 2, 9 × 10, 90 × 1, 16 × 5
14. 75 = 25 × 3, 75 × 1, 15 × 5
15. 32 = 4 × 8, 16 × 2, 32 × 1

II.2 (1 point per correct answer); total points: 15
1. 1 meter = 3.28 feet
2. 1 liter = 1.0567 quarts
3. 45 milometers = 279.45 miles
4. 4 bags; 88.184 pounds
5. 3 decagrams = 1.0581 ounces = 30 grams
6. 1.89 hectoliter = 50 gallons
7. 55 miles per hour = 8 kilometers per hour
8. 39.37 inches = 10 decimeters = 100 centimeters
9. 2 metric tons = 4409.2 pounds
10. 100 meter = 109 yards
    110 meter = 119.9 yards
    1500 meter = 1635 yards

II.3 (2 points per correct answer); total points: 24
1. B_1; B_{12} 6. A; B_2
2. B_1 7. A
3. D   8. D
4. C   9. B_2
5. K   10. C

II.4 (1 point per correct answer); total points: 11
1. Record all 8 years—1 point
2. Gave graph a title—1 point
3. Labeled left side of graph—1 point
4. Graph solution—8 points

Projected Number of Pizzas 1978 to 1985

Number of pizzas
to be eaten

| | 1978 | 1979 | 1980 | 1981 | 1982 | 1983 | 1984 | 1985 |

II.5 (1 point per correct answer); total points: 12
1. e 80kg
2. d .5kg
3. h 2.5kg
4. f 1kg
5. b 5kg
6. j 25kg
7. l 1600kg
8. i 160g
9. c 100kg
10. g 310g
11. a 36g
12. k 3¾ liter

II.6 (2 points for each part of the graph); total points: 24
1. School D (2 points)
2. Jr. High E (2 points)

Victories   Junior High School Victories (Name)

14

12

10

8

6

4

     A   B   C   D   E   F
                  Schools

II.7 (1 point per correct answer); total points: 31

Items purchased	Cash price	Monthly Payment Plan			Finance charge	Difference between cash & installment price
		$ Per month	Number of months	Total		
EXAMPLE: Typewriter	$ 140	$ 7	24	$ 168	$ 28	$ 28
1. Stereo	250	10	30	300	50	50
2. T.V.	390	24	20	480	90	90
3. Table	190	11	20	220	30	30
4. Clothes	180	17	12	204	24	24
5. Chairs	220	15	18	270	50	50
6. Washer	285	33	10	330	45	45
7. Dryer	220	10	22	220	20	20
8. Moped	375	22	20	440	65	65
9. Boat	1850	100	22	2200	350	350
10. Car	4200	138	36	4968	768	768

The difference between the *cash* price and the *installment* price is the same as the *finance charge*.

II.8 (points listed below); total points: 12
1. The boy was told to mow his lawn. (3 points, 8 words or less; 2 points, 9 or 10 words; 1 point, 11–16 words)
2. The students ate their lunch from their lunch boxes. (3 points, 9 words or less; 2 points, 10–12 words; 1 point, 14-21 words)
3. The girl read the book. (3 points, 5 words or less; 2 points, 6–8 words; 1 point, 9 or more words)
4. The airplane took off. (3 points, 4 words; 2 points 5–7 words; 1 point, 8 or more words)

	What	Where	When	How	Who
1. the doctor					✓
2. Friday at the game		✓	✓		
3. door closed softly	✓			✓	
4. earlier that morning			✓		
5. hurry to school	✓	✓			
6. say it faster				✓	
7. across the state		✓			
8. early Thanksgiving day			✓		
9. over the barn		✓			
10. my teacher					✓
11. maybe by tonight			✓		
12. a caterpillar, crawling	✓			✓	
13. waves in the ocean	✓	✓			
14. the red firetruck	✓				
15. the mailman					✓
16. at six o'clock			✓		
17. very slowly				✓	
18. the yellow cat	✓				
19. today at school		✓	✓		
20. by coasting downhill				✓	

III.1 (2 points per correct answer; 2 points for each bar on the graph); total points: 24
1. Jimmy
2. Dick
3. 90
4. 70
5. 80
6. 85

Holiday Tournament Point Graph

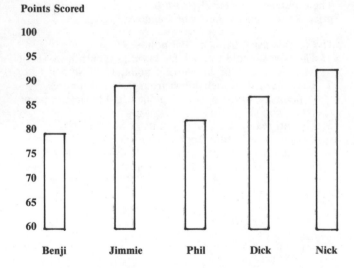

Points Scored

III.2 (3 points per correct answer); total points: 30

1. 12 cm		**6.** 8 cm	
2. 8 cm		**7.** 10 cm	
3. 8 cm		**8.** 13 cm	
4. 9 cm		**9.** 29 cm	
5. 8 cm		**10.** 12 cm	

III.3 (1 point per correctly placed planet); total points: 9

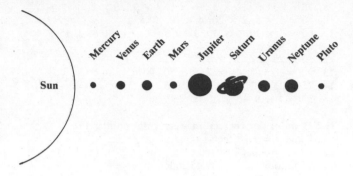

III.4 (1 point per correct answer); total points: 10
1. George
2. 12
3. One point for each line labeled correctly.
4. Labeled Home Runs: 1 point.
5. Labeled the side with the names of players: 1 point.
6. Named graph: 1 point.

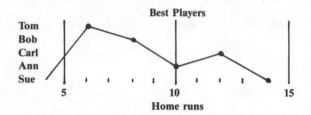

III.5 (2 points per correct answer); total points: 10
1. 80 quarters
2. $15.50
3. 130 dimes
4. $11.25
5. $10

III.6 (1 point per correct answer); total points: 10
1. Mary   6. Tim
2. Elizabeth   7. Joe
3. 30   8. 28
4. 32   9. 30
5. 25   10. 24

III.7 (points are listed); total points: 12
1. 4′9″: 1 point   5. 5′2″: 1 point
2. 5′1″: 1 point   6. 5′5″: 1 point
3. 4′11″: 1 point   7. 5′9″: 2 points
4. 0 (dark!): 3 points   8. 4′11″: 2 points

7. 1 point difference

III.8 (2 points per correct step); total points: 30
Stacie's solution
1. Stacie first filled the 5-quart jar.
2. From the 5-quart jar she filled the 3-quart jar.
3. She then emptied the 3 quart jar.
4. She then poured the 2 quarts left in the 5-quart jar into the 3-quart jar.
5. She refilled the 5-quart jar.
6. She poured 1 quart from the 5-quart jar into the 3-quart jar, filling it up.
7. She was left with exactly 4 quarts, or 1 gallon.

Kacie's Solution
1. Kacie first filled the 3-quart jar.
2. She dumped the 3 quarts into the 5-quart jar.
3. She refilled the 3-quart jar again.
4. She poured 2 of the 3 quarts into the 5-quart jar, filling it up and leaving 1 quart in the 3-quart jar.
5. She emptied the 5-quart jar.
6. She dumped the 1 quart left in the 3-quart jar into the empty 5-quart jar.
7. She refilled the 3-quart jar.
8. Kacie dumped the 3 quarts into the 5-quart jar which already contained 1 quart ending up with 4 quarts, or 1 gallon.

III.9 (1 point per correct answer); total points: 12
1. *ocean* should be *air*
2. *distance* should be *temperature*
3. *food* should be *silverware*
4. T
5. T
6. *in* should be *off*
7. T
8. *wall* should be *floor*
9. T
10. *bold* should be *shy*
11. T
12. T

IV.1 (points as listed); total points: 17
1. *Square:* 1 point

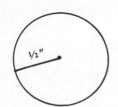

2. 2 points

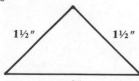

3. 2 points

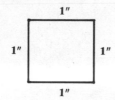

4. 2 points

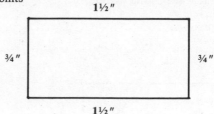

5. 2 points

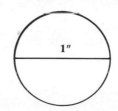

6. 6 points

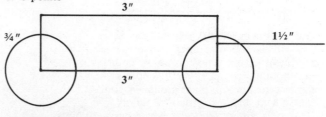

IV.2 (1 point per correct answer; titles may vary); total points: 31
1. Baseball
  A. Equipment
    1. bat
    2. ball
    3. glove
  B. Positions
    1. pitcher
    2. catcher
    3. infielders
    4. outfielders

2. Four Food Groups
  A. Fruit and Vegetable Group
    1. apple
    2. lettuce
    3. bean
    4. orange
  B. Grain Group
    1. bread
    2. cereal
    3. rice
    4. macaroni
  C. Meat Group
    1. beef
    2. chicken
    3. fish
    4. pork
  D. Milk Group
    1. ice cream
    2. cheese
    3. milk
    4. yogurt

IV.3 (Points as listed); total points: 12
1. 4 (2 points)
2. 10 (2 points)
3. 8 (2 points)
4. 16 (2 points)
5. 4 points

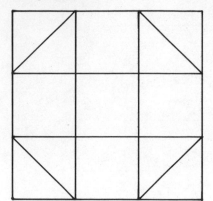

IV.4 (Points as listed); total points: 42
Sue: milk group—2 points
Bill: meat group; cereal group—4 points
Jan: nothing: complete diet—2 points
Kacia: cereal group, meat group—4 points
Clark: fruit and veg. group—2 points
Dick: milk group, fruit and veg. group—4 points

Give 2 points for each food-group item listed for each meal.

IV.5 (Points as listed); total points: 50

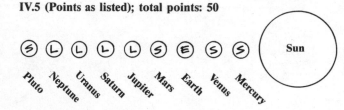

16 points for correct sizes of planets
 2 points for sun size
 2 points for straight line
18 points for correct order
_____
38 points for correct order

1. 4 (2 points)
2. 4—2 points
3. Neptune—2 points
4. Neptune—2 points
5. Saturn; 17 (2 points each)

IV.6 (2 points per correct answer); total points: 36
1. stimulate
2. eradicate
3. hinder
4. weigh
5. stun
6. sear
7. meddle
8. infuriate
9. hoist
10. inspire
11. exterminate
12. resist
13. deliberate
14. paralyze
15. char
16. intrude
17. enrage
18. heave

IV.7 (2 points per correct answer); total points: 40
1. h
2. h
3. s
4. h
5. h
6. h
7. h
8. h
9. a
10. h
11. h
12. a
13. h
14. s
15. h
16. s
17. s
18. a
19. a
20. s

IV.8 (2 points per correct answer); total points: 20
1. Thomas
2. 5
3. 7 years
4. 10
5. 2 years
6. tomorrow; 12 years old
7. 13
8. 33
9. 46

IV.9 (2 points per correct answer); total points: 20
1. iris
2. ash
3. fine
4. nails
5. chest
6. cold
7. plant
8. squash
9. saw
10. ruler

V.1 (2 points per correctly labeled answer); total points: 12

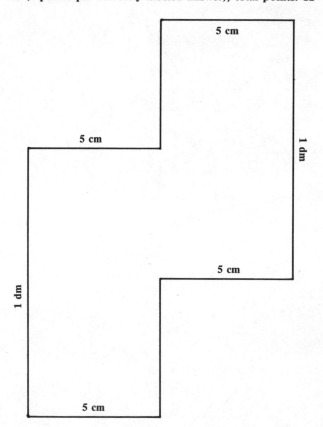

V.2 (1 point per correct answer); total points: 20

1.
| 1 | 3 | 5 | 7 | 9 |

| 2 |

| 4 |

| 6 |

| 8 |

| 10 |

2.
| 2 | 1 | 3 |

| 4 |

| 6 |

| 5 |

| 8 |

| 9 | 7 | 10 |

V.3 (1 point per correct answer); total points: 36

A good decoder always looks for a system. Can you figure out our system? Your answers to the questions below will tell us if you figured out our system. Okay, Sherlock, good luck!

1. 3 times
2. 6
3. every 3 letters

V.4 (2 points per correct answer); total points: 52

Human beings	Animals	Man-made things	Plants
h	a	d	c
j	b	i	e
l	f	k	j
n	g	r	o
o	j	s	q
q	o		
s	p		
	q		
	t		

V.5 (3 points per correct answer); total points: 12

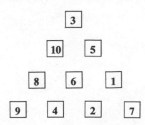

	3	
10		5
8	6	1
9	4	2	7

V.6 Total points: 12

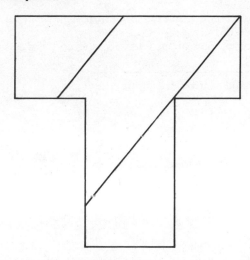

V.7 (1 point per word); total points: 21

V.8 (10 points for a correct figure); total points: 12
(2 points for naming figure)

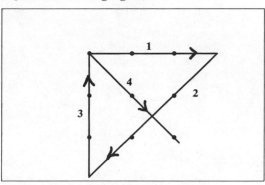

V.9 (1 point per correct answer); total points: 4

1. computer   3. brain
2. elephant   4. atom

VI.1 (The activities in this section are *not* rated by points.)
Suggested interpretations:

1. Be nice to those who provide for you.
2. When something needs to be done, do it!
3. Keep moving.
4. What you do is more important than what you say.
5. Some things and people are all "show."
6. Some people just don't want to change their ways.
7. Beware of shady people.
8. Choose appropriate friends.
9. Some people talk a lot but do little.
10. Just do what needs to be done and get it over with.
11. If you really need something, you can figure out how to get it.
12. When you share interests with other people, you have something in common.

VI.2 *Suggested interpretations:*

1. Yes
   Next mission is to be friendship offering.
   Have visited many times before.
   Wanted to know about Earth so as to do the right thing.
2. Yes
   Many years of research.
   Data used to make friendship offering.
3. Yes
   Hid in the desert.
   Used disguise.
   Have not yet made official contact.
4. Yes
   Old disguise: clothes, car, language.
   Date from 25 years ago.
5. Yes
   Secret research ends.
   Open new venture of friendship.
6. Yes
   Years of research.
   Data gathering.
   Plans based on research.

VI.3

Suggested responses:
1. F
2. F
3. F
4. F
5. F
6. F
7. T
8. F
9. F
10. F

VI.4

Suggested responses:
1. F
2. O
3. O
4. F
5. O
6. O
7. F
8. O
9. F
10. O
11. F
12. O
13. F
14. O

VI.5

Each question should have a yes or no response and a Pro and Con list.

VI.6

Suggested responses: (All answers are acceptable if the students have support from the paragraph for their answers or have presented information to support their judgments):

1. yes	6. yes
2. yes	7. no
3. no	8. yes
4. no	9. no
5. yes	10. yes

VI.7

All answers acceptable:
1. + John's pet was a *soft and cuddly* puppy.
2. + Grandma was a very *lovable* person.
3. − The *sharp and jagged* metal was a danger to the playing children.
4. − The old man gave us the *evil eye* when we cut across his lawn.
5. + Mr. Johnson was liked by everyone because he was such a *decent, kind, and caring* person.
6. + Jenny was liked by all the fourth-grade students because she was always *considerate and helpful* to everyone.
7. 0 The soup was very *bland* and no one wanted seconds.
8. − The *teary eyed* child ran to her mother for comfort.
9. + The slow burning fireplace made the family room a *comfortable and warm* room on a wintery night.
10. − The *dumpy and messy* house was an embarrassment to the neighborhood.

VI.8

Suggested responses:
1. a hard worker;
   studied hard; achieved at an early age; used what he learned in his job; others
2. would study the problem; would listen; would help talk it out; others
3. good listener; concerned person; others liked him; studies the problem before advising; others
4. concerned about them; tried to understand them; listened to them; had a quiet approach
5. He became a great galaxy leader. He was admired by everyone. He became a great peacemaker. Others turned to him for help. He united the whole galaxy. He became a friend to everyone. He became a great hero.

VI.9

Correct responses and suggested reasons:
1. A Both are the *results* of each one's work.
2. A Both a *net* and a *trap* are used to capture an animal.
3. D We *laugh* because something is *humorous*. We don't *shiver* because of our feet but probably because we're *cold* or *scared*.
4. A *Television* is a kind of *entertainment,* and *jogging* is a kind of *exercise.*
5. A *Rough* and *soft* are characteristics.
6. A You need *ink* to make a *pen* write and you need *ribbon* (cartridge) to make a *typewriter* type.
7. A A *brush* goes on your *teeth,* and *polish* goes on your *shoes.*
8. A A *filthy* place usually leads to *disease,* and *speeding* usually leads to an *accident.*